JUL 2013

# TEAM SPIRIT ®

## SMART BOOKS FOR YOUNG FANS

# THE GREEN BAY PACKERS

BY
**MARK STEWART**

NORWOOD HOUSE PRESS

CHICAGO, ILLINOIS

Norwood House Press
P.O. Box 316598
Chicago, Illinois 60631

For information regarding Norwood House Press, please visit our website at:
www.norwoodhousepress.com or call 866-565-2900.

The memorabilia and artifacts pictured in this book are presented for educational and informational purposes,
and come from the collection of the author.

Editor: Mike Kennedy
Designer: Ron Jaffe
Project Management: Black Book Partners, LLC.
Special thanks to Topps, Inc.

Library of Congress Cataloging-in-Publication Data

Stewart, Mark, 1960-
    The Green Bay Packers / by Mark Stewart.
        p. cm. -- (Team spirit)
    Includes bibliographical references and index.
    Summary: "Team Spirit Football edition featuring the Green Bay Packers
that chronicles the history and accomplishments of the team. Includes access
to the Team Spirit website which provides additional information and
photos"--Provided by publisher.
    ISBN 978-1-59953-523-4 (library edition : alk. paper) -- ISBN
978-1-60357-465-5 (ebook)
    1. Green Bay Packers (Football team)--History--Juvenile literature. I.
Title.
    GV956.G7S74 2012
    796.332'640977561--dc23
                                                            2012012310

Manufactured in the United States of America in North Mankato, Minnesota.
205N—082012

**COVER PHOTO**: Aaron Rodgers leads the Packers onto the field before a 2011 game.

# Table of Contents

**ABOUT OUR GLOSSARY**

In this book, there may be several words that you are reading for the first time. Some are sports words, some are new vocabulary words, and some are familiar words that are used in an unusual way. All of these words are defined on page 46. Throughout the book, sports words appear in **bold type**. Regular vocabulary words appear in ***bold italic type***.

# Meet the Packers

**W**hen people say that football has become a global sport, they mean that the top teams and players have fans all over the world. That explains why Green Bay—a town in Wisconsin with just over 100,000 people—is known to hundreds of millions in every corner of the planet. Green Bay is where the Packers play, and no team has done more to make football popular.

The Packers have been a championship club since the 1920s. They play for the sport's most *demanding* owners— their fans. Other teams are owned by companies or a small group of business people. The Packers are different. Over the years, thousands of people have bought small parts of the team and own it together.

This book tells the story of the Packers. They win the old-fashioned way—with speed, power, and toughness. They don't have much choice. Whenever the players look into the stands, they know their bosses are watching!

Clay Matthews strikes his famous "Predator" pose. Green Bay fans love to cheer for players with his passion for the game.

# Glory Days

**T**he Packers might not exist if not for a case of ***tonsillitis***. In 1919, Curly Lambeau fell ill while in college and decided to return home to Green Bay to recover from his throat infection. Lambeau had been a football star in high school. George Calhoun knew all about him. Calhoun was one of the newspaper reporters who wrote about Lambeau's heroics. One day, the two men met by chance, and in no time they decided to form a ***professional*** football team. The Indian Packing Company put up $500 for equipment and uniforms, so Lambeau named the club the Indian Packers. After each game, the fans put bills and coins in a hat and the players divided the money.

While the Packers earned a ***reputation*** for their fine play, a new football league

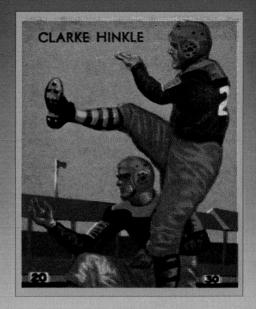

CLARKE HINKLE

was being organized. Green Bay joined in 1921. A year later, the league changed its name to the **National Football League (NFL)**. Over the next few years, Lambeau built an excellent squad. It included Red Dunn, Lavvie Dilweg, Mike Michalske, Cal Hubbard, Verne Lewellen, and Dick O'Donnell. Green Bay had a winning record in each of its first 12 seasons. The team finished the season as the NFL champion each year from 1929 to 1931.

The Packers continued their success through the 1930s and into the 1940s. Lambeau made the forward pass an important part of his team's playbook at a time when the rules greatly favored the running game. He was able to do so because he had two strong-armed quarterbacks—Arnie Herber and Cecil Isbell—and a talented receiver named Don Hutson.

Another star of this *era* for Green Bay was Clarke Hinkle. He did everything well. On offense, he was a powerful runner and good passer. He was also one of the league's top punters and kickers. Hinkle was a defensive star as well. The Packers won the NFL championship in 1936, 1939, and 1944.

**LEFT**: Curly Lambeau
**ABOVE**: Clarke Hinkle

After struggling during the 1950s, the Packers returned to the top of the NFL in the 1960s. Their coach was Vince Lombardi. He demanded perfection from his players. They practiced plays until they knew them in their sleep. Green Bay captured

five NFL titles from 1961 to 1967, including a victory in the first **Super Bowl**.

These great teams depended on a handful of stars, including quarterback Bart Starr and running backs Jim Taylor and Paul Hornung. However, the key to victory was teamwork. When the Packers had the ball, the offensive line controlled the field. On defense, Green Bay's linebackers and defensive backs were always in the right place at the right time. No fewer than 10 players who played for Lombardi made it to the **Hall of Fame**. Included among them were Herb Adderley, Willie Davis, Forrest Gregg, Henry Jordan, Ray Nitschke, Jim Ringo, and Willie Wood.

**LEFT**: Paul Hornung signed this photo taken during warm-ups for Super Bowl I.
**ABOVE**: The Packers carry Vince Lombardi off the field after Super Bowl II.

The Packers had their ups and downs in the 1970s and 1980s. Several stars wore the green and gold, including quarterback Lynn Dickey, receiver James Lofton, running back John Brockington, kicker Chester Marcol, and linebacker Fred Carr. Green Bay went to the **playoffs** just twice during this time, in 1972 and 1982.

The team started winning again after Mike Holmgren became head coach in 1992. One of Holmgren's first moves was to make rifle-armed Brett Favre his starting quarterback. Favre played with great joy and *intensity*. He guided the Packers to the playoffs in 10 of his 16 seasons and led the NFL in touchdown passes four times.

Joining Favre in the huddle were many other top players, including running back Ahman Green and receivers Sterling Sharpe, Antonio Freeman, Robert Brooks, and Donald Driver. Green Bay's defense starred Reggie White, LeRoy Butler, Gilbert Brown,

Santana Dotson, Darren Sharper, and Aaron Kampman. With Favre in charge, the Packers went to the Super Bowl twice and won their 10th NFL championship in 1997.

The Packers returned to the top of the NFL more than a *decade* later. By this time, Green Bay's field leader was quarterback Aaron Rodgers. He was the heart of a rebuilt team that included young pass-catching stars Jordy Nelson, Greg Jennings, and Jermichael Finley. Charles Woodson, A.J. Hawk, Clay Matthews, Nick Collins, and Tramon Williams led the defense. The Packers got hot at the end of the 2010 season and rolled through the playoffs. In Super Bowl XLV, Green Bay beat the Pittsburgh Steelers.

A year later, the Packers went 15–1, and Rodgers had one of the greatest seasons of any quarterback in NFL history. Just as in the old days, Green Bay fans now begin each season expecting their team to challenge for the championship.

**LEFT**: Brett Favre led the Packers for 16 seasons.
**ABOVE**: Aaron Rodgers took over for Favre and won a championship.

# Home Turf

The Packers play their home games in one of football's most famous stadiums, Lambeau Field. When it first opened in 1957, it was called City Stadium. Eight years later, it was renamed Lambeau Field in honor of Curly Lambeau.

No NFL team has played in its home stadium longer than the Packers. From the outside, Lambeau Field reminds fans of old-time stadiums with its "retro" building features. On the inside, many parts of Lambeau Field have been updated. That includes the playing surface, which is now a mix of natural grass and *artificial* turf. In 2012, two huge high-definition video boards were added behind each end zone.

## BY THE NUMBERS

- *The Packers' stadium has 73,142 seats.*
- *The stadium includes a five-story building that houses the 25,000-square-foot Packers Hall of Fame.*
- *Two statues stand outside the stadium. One is of Lambeau and the other is of Vince Lombardi.*

Lambeau Field has been home to the Packers for more than 50 years.

# Dressed for Success

T he Packers' uniform is one of the best known in all of sports. But dark green and gold weren't always the Green Bay colors. Originally, the team wore blue and gold, the same colors as the University of Notre Dame at the time. Fans often called the Packers the "Bay Blues."

The team changed its colors to green and gold after Vince Lombardi became the coach in 1959. Two years later, the team began to feature its famous *G logo* on the sides of its helmets. It was designed by the club's equipment manager, Dad Brashier.

The Packers haven't changed their uniforms much since the 1960s. The stripes on the jersey and pants have been altered slightly, and the players now wear green socks. But the current uniform is very similar to the one that Lombardi chose more than 50 years ago.

PACKERS

**Bill Howton**
END      GREEN BAY PACKERS

**LEFT**: Donald Driver wears the green and gold that the Packers have used since 1959.   **ABOVE**: This trading card of Billy Howton shows the Packers' earlier blue uniform.

# We Won!

From 1920 to 1932, the NFL did not play a championship game. Instead, the team with the best record at the end of the season was crowned the league champion. During this time, the Packers won the title three years in a row—1929, 1930, and 1931. These great teams were led by coach Curly Lambeau. He assembled a talented roster that included Johnny "Blood" McNally, Cal Hubbard, Mike Michalske, Verne Lewellen, Lavvie Dilweg, and Arnie Herber.

Lambeau coached the Packers through the 1930s and 1940s. They played in four championship games during that period. In 1936, Green Bay beat the Boston Redskins in the title game. Herber completed several long passes to McNally and star receiver Don Hutson. The Packers won easily, 21–6.

Green Bay played the New York Giants for the NFL title in 1938 and 1939. The Giants won the first meeting. The Packers turned the tables the following year with a 27–0 victory. In 1944, the Packers and the Giants played again for the championship. The result was another Green Bay victory, 14–7.

Jim Taylor and Paul Hornung lift Vince Lombardi off the ground after Green Bay's 1965 victory over the Cleveland Browns.

The Packers and Giants met for the NFL crown two more times. Coach Vince Lombardi led Green Bay to a 37–0 victory in 1961. Bart Starr threw three touchdown passes, and Paul Hornung scored 19 points as a running back and kicker. A year later, the teams had a rematch. Green Bay won 16–7, thanks to another great defensive effort. Ray Nitschke, Willie Wood, and Herb Adderley led the charge.

In 1965, the Packers faced the Cleveland Browns for the NFL title. Green Bay had its hands full with running back Jim Brown. Lombardi ordered Nitschke to "shadow" the powerful runner on every play. The plan worked, and Green Bay won 23–12.

In 1966 and 1967, the Packers defeated the Dallas Cowboys for the NFL title. Both contests were very exciting, but unlike other seasons, there was one more game to be played. After years as rivals, the NFL and the **American Football League (AFL)** agreed to work

together for the good of professional football. The first step was an AFL–NFL championship game—which everyone soon called the Super Bowl.

The Packers beat the Kansas City Chiefs in Super Bowl I. Starr was named the game's **Most Valuable Player (MVP)**. Green Bay defended its title in Super Bowl II against the Oakland Raiders. The Packers won easily, and Starr was honored again as MVP.

Green Bay fans had to wait a long time for their third Super Bowl trophy. It came in 1997. Brett Favre led the Packers into battle against the New England Patriots in Super Bowl XXXI. He threw long touchdown passes to Andre Rison and Antonio Freeman in the first half. But the player who gave New England the most trouble was Desmond Howard. He returned four kickoffs and six punts for

244 yards, including a thrilling 99-yard score. The Packers won 35–21, and Howard was voted MVP.

In 2008, Aaron Rodgers took over for Favre as the team's starting quarterback. By 2010, he had developed into one of the NFL's top passers. The Green Bay defense also improved. Its leaders included Clay Matthews and Charles Woodson. The Packers swept through the playoffs to earn a trip to Super Bowl XLV.

Green Bay met the Pittsburgh Steelers for the championship. In the first half, Rodgers connected with Greg Jennings and Jordy Nelson for touchdowns. Nick Collins **intercepted** a pass and ran it in for a score to increase Green Bay's lead. The Steelers fought back, but Rodgers responded with another touchdown pass to Jennings. The Packers added a **field goal** and then stopped Pittsburgh in the final two minutes for a 31–25 win. Green Bay celebrated its fourth Super Bowl victory and 11th NFL title.

**LEFT**: Desmond Howard gets a hug after his great Super Bowl performance.
**ABOVE**: Greg Jennings catches a pass from Aaron Rodgers.

# Go-To Guys

To be a true star in the NFL, you need more than fast feet and a big body. You have to be a "go-to guy"—someone the coach wants on the field at the end of a big game. Packers fans have had a lot to cheer about over the years, including these great stars …

## THE PIONEERS

### DON HUTSON                    Receiver/Defensive Back

• BORN: 1/31/1913   • DIED: 6/26/1997   • PLAYED FOR TEAM: 1935 TO 1945

Don Hutson was the NFL's first great receiver. He was very fast and usually caught passes at full speed. Hutson was the first receiver to be regularly double-covered. He was also an excellent defensive player.

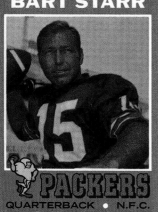

### BART STARR                    Quarterback

• BORN: 1/9/1934   • PLAYED FOR TEAM: 1956 TO 1971

Bart Starr made winning look easy. He was a calm and confident leader who always seemed to make the right call in the huddle. Starr was the NFL's top passer three times and the MVP of the first two Super Bowls.

## PAUL HORNUNG — Running Back/Kicker

• BORN: 12/23/1935   • PLAYED FOR TEAM: 1957 TO 1962 & 1964 TO 1966

Paul Hornung was a scoring machine. He could run, pass, catch, and kick—and usually saved his best plays for the key moments in a game. In 1960, Hornung scored 176 points in 14 games.

## JIM TAYLOR — Running Back

• BORN: 9/20/1935   • PLAYED FOR TEAM: 1958 TO 1966

Jim Taylor was the perfect fullback. He was a great blocker, a punishing runner, and an expert at turning short passes into long gains. Taylor was the man the Packers turned to late in games, when every yard and first down was crucial.

## RAY NITSCHKE — Linebacker

• BORN: 12/29/1936   • DIED: 3/8/1998   • PLAYED FOR TEAM: 1958 TO 1972

Ray Nitschke was the man in the middle of Green Bay's great defenses of the 1960s. He was the team's hardest hitter and one of its best athletes. Nitschke was the star of the 1962 NFL Championship Game.

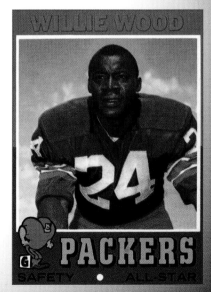

## WILLIE WOOD — Defensive Back

• BORN: 12/23/1936   • PLAYED FOR TEAM: 1960 TO 1971

Willie Wood was a quarterback in college, but no NFL team **drafted** him. He became a safety as a **rookie** with the Packers and put his passing knowledge to work on defense. Wood led the league in interceptions in 1962.

**LEFT**: Bart Starr   **RIGHT**: Willie Wood

### JAMES LOFTON                                    Receiver

- BORN: 7/5/1956    • PLAYED FOR TEAM: 1978 TO 1986

James Lofton had sure hands and a track star's speed. No one in the NFL was harder to cover on deep passes. Lofton was named to the **Pro Bowl** seven times in his nine seasons with the Packers. He was voted into the Hall of Fame in 2003.

### STERLING SHARPE                                 Receiver

- BORN: 4/6/1965    • PLAYED FOR TEAM: 1988 TO 1994

Any pass that Sterling Sharpe could touch, he usually caught. He was fast and tough and almost impossible to stop on short passes. Sharpe was at the top of his game when a neck injury forced him to retire.

### BRETT FAVRE                                     Quarterback

- BORN: 10/10/1969    • PLAYED FOR TEAM: 1992 TO 2007

Few quarterbacks have scared opposing defenses more than Brett Favre. From 1994 to 1998, he threw 176 touchdown passes and led the Packers to two Super Bowls. Favre was a great competitor who started more than 200 games in a row.

### REGGIE WHITE                                Defensive Lineman

- BORN: 12/19/1961    • DIED: 12/26/2004    • PLAYED FOR TEAM: 1993 TO 1998

When Reggie White joined the Packers in 1993, he turned them into a great defensive team. His ability to stop the run and rush the quarterback made all of his teammates better. White retired with the most **sacks** in NFL history.

## AARON RODGERS Quarterback

- BORN: 12/2/1983    • FIRST YEAR WITH TEAM: 2005

Aaron Rodgers waited on the bench for three years before the Packers decided it was time for him to replace Brett Favre at quarterback. His patience paid off. Rodgers was the first player to throw for 4,000 yards in each of his first two years as a starter. In 2011, he led the Packers to a 15–1 record and was named NFL MVP.

## CHARLES WOODSON Defensive Back

- BORN: 10/7/1976    • FIRST YEAR WITH TEAM: 2006

Charles Woodson continued Green Bay's *tradition* of great defensive backs. In his first season with the Packers, he had eight interceptions. Woodson was selected to the Pro Bowl four years in a row starting in 2008.

## CLAY MATTHEWS Linebacker

- BORN: 5/14/1986    • FIRST YEAR WITH TEAM: 2009

Clay Matthews was picked to play in the Pro Bowl in each of his first three seasons. His ferocious tackling helped him become an **All-Pro** in 2010. Matthews's father and grandfather both played in the NFL, and his brother Casey was drafted by the Philadelphia Eagles in 2011.

**RIGHT**: Charles Woodson

# Calling the Shots

No job in football is quite like being the head coach of the Packers. The hopes and dreams of Green Bay ride on every game. But the team also has millions of fans around the world. That's a lot of pressure! The man who set the stage for every Green Bay coach was Curly Lambeau. He was tough on his players, but he also knew how to get the very best they had to give.

Vince Lombardi was even tougher than Lambeau. One player joked that Lombardi treated everyone the same—like dogs! No one complained about his results, however. In each of Lombardi's nine seasons, the Packers had a winning record. The secret to Lombardi's success was how he got his players to work together as one. He drew up plays that succeeded only if each player did his job to perfection. When this happened, the Packers were impossible to stop. Lombardi loved to run a play called the Power Sweep. In slow motion, it almost looked like ballet!

**LEFT**: Mike Holmgren thinks about his next move.
**RIGHT**: Mike McCarthy talks things over with Aaron Rodgers.

Like Lambeau and Lombardi, Mike Holmgren could be tough on his players. But he was also friendly and fatherly. Holmgren coached Green Bay from 1992 to 1998 and led the Packers back to the Super Bowl. Holmgren was good at making a winning game plan, and he worked hard to earn the trust and confidence of his players. The Packers were one of football's best teams every year he coached them.

One of Holmgren's assistants was Mike McCarthy. He coached the Green Bay quarterbacks, including Brett Favre and Aaron Rodgers. In 2006, McCarthy became the head coach. He had learned a lot from Holmgren. In 2010, McCarthy led the Packers to the NFL title in Super Bowl XLV.

# One Great Day

When the temperature drops and the wind whips off Lake Michigan, Lambeau Field can be an unpleasant place to play football. No wonder that the coldest day in Packers history was also their greatest. Indeed, the weather for the 1967 NFL Championship

Game between the Packers and the Dallas Cowboys was worse than anyone could remember. The thermometer read 13 degrees below zero at kickoff. The wind made it feel 30 degrees colder. No matter what the players did, they could not get warm.

Still, there was a game to be played. The Packers started quickly. Bart Starr threw two touchdown passes to Boyd Dowler in the first half. Dallas, however, recovered two Green Bay fumbles and scored twice to cut the Packers' lead to 14–10. Early in the fourth quarter, Dan Reeves of the Cowboys took a handoff and surprised the Packers when he stopped and threw a 50-yard touchdown pass.

The Packers trailed 17–14 with under five minutes left. They began the game's final drive on their own 32-yard line. Starr called a mixture of running plays and short passes and moved the ball all the way to the 1-yard line with less than 60 seconds on the clock. He handed off to Donny Anderson twice, but the Cowboys stopped him both times.

With the seconds ticking down and no timeouts left, the Packers had a chance to tie the game with a field goal. Instead, Starr called a third run into the line. It was a gamble, because Green Bay had no way to stop the clock if the play failed. This time Starr carried the ball himself. He ran to the right and dove through a hole created by two of his linemen, Jerry Kramer and Ken Bowman. The Packers won 21–17. Forever after, this amazing game would be called the "Ice Bowl."

**LEGEND HAS IT** that the Packers are. In the late 1950s, Vince Lombardi wanted the team to form a closer relationship with its young fans. He noticed that many fans rode their bikes to the team's training camp during the summer. Lombardi told the kids that his players would ride the bikes from the locker room to the practice field. It is a team tradition that continues to this day.

ABOVE: The Packers are the biggest things on wheels.
RIGHT: Mason Crosby lines up a field goal.

# Were the 2010 Packers the most competitive team in NFL history?

**LEGEND HAS IT** that they were. In the NFL, the key to success is keeping games close. If you can stay within a touchdown of your opponents, then you always have a chance to win. In 2010, Green Bay won 10 games, but none of the team's six losses was by more than four points. Even more amazing, the Packers never trailed at any time—in any game—by more than seven points. No team had done that since the NFL season went from 14 games to 16 games in 1978.

# Who was Green Bay's greatest long-distance kicker?

**LEGEND HAS IT** that Mason Crosby was. In his first NFL game, Crosby booted a game-winning field goal from 53 yards away with just two seconds left. No rookie had ever done that on the first weekend of the NFL season. In 2010, Crosby set a team record with a 56-yard field goal. In October of 2011, he broke his own record with a booming 58-yarder. The kick would have been good from at least 65 yards!

# It Really Happened

Vince Lombardi and his 35-year-old receiver Max McGee had what some people call a "love-hate" relationship. The super-strict coach loved McGee's ability to come off the bench and make big plays—and hated the sneaky ways McGee had of breaking his rules. The evening before the first Super Bowl, Lombardi warned his players that they had to be in bed by 11 PM. McGee was in bed on time.

However, as soon as Lombardi went to sleep, McGee was on his way out of the hotel and into Los Angeles, where a night of Super Bowl parties awaited him. The receiver was not worried about the next day's game. Lombardi wasn't planning on using him, and McGee was set to retire after the game. He had played 11 seasons and just wanted to enjoy his last night as a Packer. In the locker room the next day, a weary McGee reminded receivers

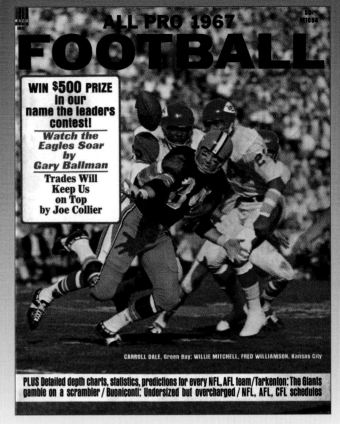

ALL PRO 1967
**FOOTBALL**

WIN **$500 PRIZE** in our name the leaders contest!

*Watch the Eagles Soar* by Gary Ballman

Trades Will Keep Us on Top by Joe Collier

CARROLL DALE, Green Bay; WILLIE MITCHELL, FRED WILLIAMSON, Kansas City

PLUS Detailed depth charts, statistics, predictions for every NFL, AFL team/Tarkenton: The Giants gamble on a scrambler / Buoniconti: Undersized but overcharged / NFL, AFL, CFL schedules

Boyd Dowler and Carroll Dale not to get hurt. "Old Max" was in no shape to play.

Sure enough, Dowler injured his shoulder early in the game. Lombardi barked out McGee's name, and the sleepy *veteran* jogged onto the field. Moments later, Bart Starr called his number. McGee cut across the middle, and Starr threw a pass that floated behind him. McGee reached back with his right arm and made a one-handed catch for a 37-yard touchdown.

McGee was now wide awake. He begged Starr to throw him the ball, and the quarterback did just that. McGee caught six more passes, scored another touchdown, and finished with 138 receiving yards. With his help, the Packers easily defeated the Kansas City Chiefs, 35–10. McGee had so much fun that he decided to play one more season. A year later, he caught a 35-yard pass in Super Bowl II!

# Team Spirit

Packers fans are known as "Cheeseheads," and they are proud of their nickname. Wisconsin is one of the nation's top cheese producers. Fans celebrate their state's history by wearing hats that look like a wedge of cheese.

That is one of many traditions that make the Packers a fun team. Another is the "Lambeau Leap." When a Green Bay player scores a touchdown at Lambeau Field, he jumps into the arms of fans sitting in the stands just behind each end zone. LeRoy Butler was the first Packer to do the Lambeau Leap, in 1993.

Why do the Packers have such a strong bond with their fans? Because the fans own the team! Three times, the club was close to going out of business. The community saved the Packers with financial donations. Today, more than 100,000 people own a part of the team.

**LEFT**: A Cheesehead watches the action during a Packers game.
**ABOVE**: LeRoy Butler does the Lambeau Leap.

# Timeline

In this timeline, each Super Bowl is listed under the year it was played. Remember that the Super Bowl is held early in the year and is actually part of the previous season. For example, Super Bowl XLVI was played on February 5, 2012, but it was the championship of the 2011 NFL season.

## 1929
Green Bay wins its first championship.

## 1949
Tony Canadeo becomes the first Packer to rush for 1,000 yards.

## 1919
The team is formed with help from a local meat-packing company.

## 1942
Don Hutson sets NFL receiving records with 74 catches and 17 touchdowns.

## 1967
The Packers win the first Super Bowl.

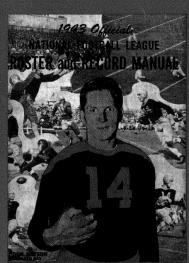

Don Hutson's great 1942 season got him on the cover of the 1943 NFL Guide.

Sterling
Sharpe

Ahman
Green

## 1992
Sterling Sharpe leads NFL receivers
in catches, yards, and touchdowns.

## 2003
Ahman Green leads the NFC
with 1,883 rushing yards.

## 1980
James Lofton leads the **National
Football Conference (NFC)**
with 1,226 receiving yards.

## 1997
The Packers win
Super Bowl XXXI.

## 2011
The Packers
win their fourth
Super Bowl.

Aaron Rodgers
was the
leader of the
2011 champs.

# Fun Facts

### MANY HAPPY RETURNS

In the 2010 playoffs, the Packers returned interceptions for touchdowns in three straight games. No team had ever done that before. The Packers also scored a touchdown off an interception in the Super Bowl that season.

### TWICE AS NICE

In 2006, Aaron Kampman became the second Packer to be named Defensive Player of the Week twice in the same season. The first was Reggie White, in 1998.

### THE WRITE STUFF

Donald Driver was a record-setting receiver for the Packers. Away from the field, he was also a children's book author. The main character in his books was "Quickie." That was the nickname Donald's mom gave him when he was a boy.

**ABOVE**: Aaron Kampman takes aim at an opposing quarterback.
**RIGHT**: Bobby Dillon leaps in the air for his 1956 trading card.

## PICK-OFF ARTIST

Bobby Dillon was one of the NFL's best defensive backs in the 1950s. He intercepted 52 passes in eight seasons, despite being blind in one eye.

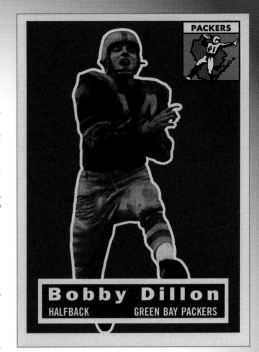

**Bobby Dillon**
HALFBACK    GREEN BAY PACKERS

## TOP RATED

In 2011, Aaron Rodgers threw for 4,643 yards with 45 touchdowns and only six interceptions. His **quarterback rating** of 122.5 was the highest in NFL history.

## ALL IN THE FAMILY

In 1989, the Packers drafted college quarterback Anthony Dilweg. His grandfather, Lavvie Dilweg, was a star on Green Bay's championship teams from 1929 to 1931.

## THUMBS UP FROM VINCE

Who was the greatest player on the championship Green Bay teams of the 1960s? Coach Vince Lombardi claimed that his right tackle, Forrest Gregg, was the "finest player" he had ever coached.

# Talking Football

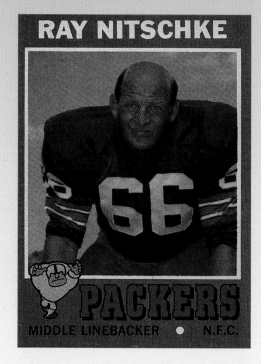

**RAY NITSCHKE**

**PACKERS**

MIDDLE LINEBACKER ● N.F.C.

"It's not whether you get knocked down, it's whether you get up."
► **Vince Lombardi,** *on what makes a winner in football and in life*

"Packer fans are nuts, man!"
► **Ray Nitschke,** *on the fun of playing and living in Green Bay*

"Coach Lombardi showed me that by working hard and using my mind, I could overcome my weakness to the point where I could be one of the best."
► **Bart Starr,** *on what helped him become a Hall of Famer*

"If I had to tell people what the Green Bay Packers of my era were all about, I'd say go back and watch that drive."
► **Jerry Kramer,** *on the way the Packers marched down the field for the game-winning touchdown in the Ice Bowl*

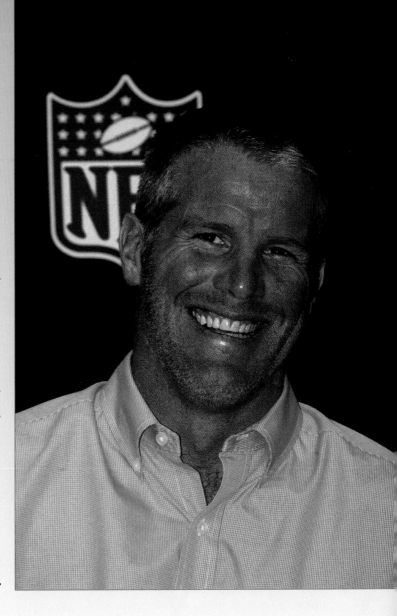

"The town, the team, it's a family."
▶ **Brett Favre,** *on what sets Green Bay and the Packers apart*

"He was very tough … exactly what we needed."
▶ **Paul Hornung,** *on Vince Lombardi's coaching style*

"For every pass I caught in a game, I caught a thousand in practice."
▶ **Don Hutson,** *on what it took to become a record-breaking receiver*

"I know the pressure I'm under. I know who I'm following."
▶ **Aaron Rodgers,** *on taking over for Brett Favre*

**LEFT**: Ray Nitschke      **ABOVE**: Brett Favre

# Great Debates

eople who root for the Packers love to compare their favorite moments, teams, and players. Some debates have been going on for years! How would you settle these classic football arguments?

### Bart Starr was the Packers' greatest quarterback ...

... because he led Green Bay to five NFL championships. How else do you measure the greatness of a team leader? Starr made the most of his talent by practicing pass plays over and over. He also studied his opponents very closely. He always knew what kind of defenses he would face each week. Vince Lombardi was a coach who demanded perfection from his players. It says a lot that he allowed Starr to call his own plays.

### The numbers say that Brett Favre was Green Bay's best ...

... because he played the same number of years for the Packers as Starr and broke almost every one of his records. Favre (      ) threw 442 touchdown passes to Starr's 152. Starr had more than 24,000 passing yards, but Favre topped 60,000. Favre completed more than 5,000 passes, while Starr completed fewer than 2,000. There is no comparison!

## Curly Lambeau was pro football's greatest coach ...

... because he was the first to make the passing game a big part of the offense. During the 1920s and 1930s, NFL rules favored running. Lambeau knew passing was the future of the game. He turned Arnie Herber and Cecil Isbell into record-breaking quarterbacks. He also helped Don Hutson become the top receiver in pro football. Lambeau coached the Packers to six championships from 1929 to 1944. Green Bay was the NFL's first true *dynasty*.

## Seriously? No one compares to Vince Lombardi ....

... because he changed the way football teams block and run. Lombardi (          ) taught his linemen how to double-team defensive players and create huge holes for the running backs. The Packers ran the same Power Sweep again and again, and opponents were helpless to stop it. Under Lombardi, all 11 players on the field worked together as one—something today's coaches are still trying to figure out!

# For the Record

The great Packers teams and players have left their marks on the record books. These are the "best of the best" …

John Jefferson

Reggie White

## PACKERS AWARD WINNERS

| WINNER | AWARD | YEAR |
|--------|-------|------|
| Don Hutson | Most Valuable Player | 1941 |
| Don Hutson | Most Valuable Player | 1942 |
| Vince Lombardi | Coach of the Year | 1959 |
| Paul Hornung | Most Valuable Player | 1961 |
| Jim Taylor | Most Valuable Player | 1962 |
| Bart Starr | Most Valuable Player | 1966 |
| Bart Starr | Super Bowl I MVP | 1967 |
| Bart Starr | Super Bowl II MVP | 1968 |
| John Brockington | Offensive Rookie of the Year | 1971 |
| Fred Carr | Pro Bowl co-MVP | 1971 |
| Willie Buchanon | Defensive Rookie of the Year | 1972 |
| John Jefferson | Pro Bowl co-MVP | 1983 |
| Lindy Infante | Coach of the Year | 1989 |
| Brett Favre | Most Valuable Player | 1995 |
| Brett Favre | Offensive Player of the Year | 1995 |
| Brett Favre | Most Valuable Player | 1996 |
| Desmond Howard | Super Bowl XXXI MVP | 1997 |
| Brett Favre | Co-Most Valuable Player | 1997 |
| Reggie White | Defensive Player of the Year | 1998 |
| Charles Woodson | Defensive Player of the Year | 2009 |
| Aaron Rodgers | Super Bowl XLV MVP | 2011 |
| Aaron Rodgers | Most Valuable Player | 2011 |

# PACKERS ACHIEVEMENTS

| ACHIEVEMENT | YEAR |
| --- | --- |
| NFL Champions | 1929 |
| NFL Champions | 1930 |
| NFL Champions | 1931 |
| Western Division Champions | 1936 |
| NFL Champions | 1936 |
| Western Division Champions | 1938 |
| Western Division Champions | 1939 |
| NFL Champions | 1939 |
| Western Division Champions | 1944 |
| NFL Champions | 1944 |
| Western Conference Champions | 1960 |
| Western Conference Champions | 1961 |
| NFL Champions | 1961 |
| Western Conference Champions | 1962 |
| NFL Champions | 1962 |
| Western Conference Champions | 1965 |
| NFL Champions | 1965 |
| Western Conference Champions | 1966 |
| NFL Champions | 1966 |
| Super Bowl I Champions | 1966* |
| Central Conference Champions | 1967 |
| NFL Champions | 1967 |
| Super Bowl II Champions | 1967* |
| NFC Central Champions | 1972 |
| NFC Central Champions | 1995 |
| NFC Central Champions | 1996 |
| NFC Champions | 1996 |
| Super Bowl XXXI Champions | 1996* |
| NFC Central Champions | 1997 |
| NFC Champions | 1997 |
| NFC North Champions | 2002 |
| NFC North Champions | 2003 |
| NFC North Champions | 2004 |
| NFC North Champions | 2007 |
| NFC North Champions | 2008 |
| NFC Champions | 2010 |
| Super Bowl XLV Champions | 2010* |
| NFC North Champions | 2011 |

*Super Bowls are played early the following year, but the game
  is counted as the championship of this season.*

**Herb ADDERLEY**
GR. BAY PACKERS • DEF. BACK

**ABOVE**: Herb Adderley starred in Green Bay's first two Super Bowls. **BELOW**: Jim Taylor appears on the cover of the team's 1965 yearbook.

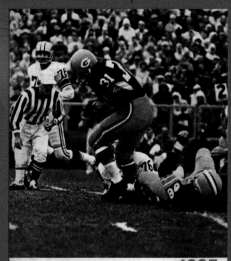

PACKERS 1965 PRESS BOOK

# Pinpoints

The history of a football team is made up of many smaller stories. These stories take place all over the map—not just in the city a team calls "home." Match the pushpins on these maps to the **Team Facts**, and you will begin to see the story of the Packers unfold!

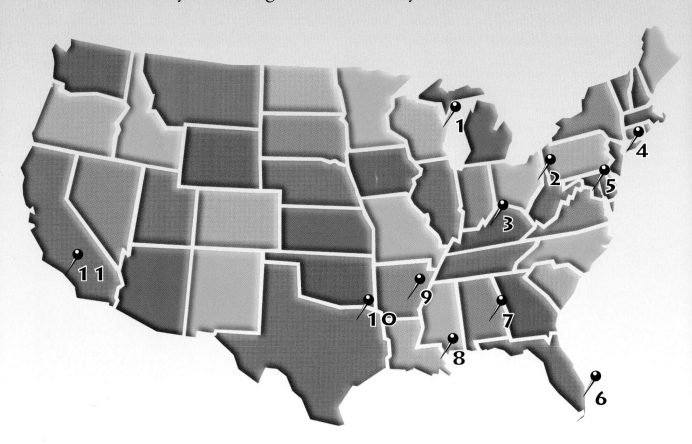

**1**   Green Bay, Wisconsin—*The Packers have played here since 1919.*

**2**   Toronto, Ohio—*Clarke Hinkle was born here.*

**3**   Louisville, Kentucky—*Paul Hornung was born here.*

**4**   Brooklyn, New York—*Vince Lombardi was born here.*

**5**   Washington, D.C.—*Willie Wood was born here.*

**6**   Miami, Florida—*The Packers won Super Bowl II here.*

**7**   Montgomery, Alabama—*Bart Starr was born here.*

**8**   New Orleans, Louisiana—*The Packers won Super Bowl XXXI here.*

**9**   Pine Bluff, Arkansas—*Don Hutson was born here.*

**10**   Birthright, Texas—*Forrest Gregg was born here.*

**11**   Los Angeles, California—*The Packers won Super Bowl I here.*

**12**   Opole, Poland—*Chester Marcol was born here.*

Forrest Gregg

# Glossary

🧠 **ALL-PRO**—An honor given to the best players at their positions at the end of each season.

🧠 **AMERICAN FOOTBALL LEAGUE (AFL)**—The football league that began play in 1960 and later merged with the NFL.

🧠 *ARTIFICIAL*—Made by people, not nature.

🧠 *DECADE*—A period of 10 years; also specific periods, such as the 1950s.

🧠 *DEMANDING*—Requiring great effort.

🧠 **DRAFTED**—Chosen from a group of the best college players. The NFL draft is held each spring.

🧠 *DYNASTY*—A family, group, or team that maintains power over time.

🧠 *ERA*—A period of time in history.

🧠 **FIELD GOAL**—A goal from the field, kicked over the crossbar and between the goal posts. A field goal is worth three points.

🧠 **HALL OF FAME**—The museum in Canton, Ohio, where football's greatest players are honored. A player voted into the Hall of Fame is sometimes called a "Hall of Famer."

🧠 *INTENSITY*—The strength and energy of a thought or action.

🧠 **INTERCEPTED**—Caught in the air by a defensive player.

🧠 *LOGO*—A symbol or design that represents a company or team.

🧠 **MOST VALUABLE PLAYER (MVP)**—The award given each year to the league's best player; also given to the best player in the Super Bowl and Pro Bowl.

🧠 **NATIONAL FOOTBALL CONFERENCE (NFC)**—One of two groups of teams that make up the NFL. The other group is known as the American Football Conference (AFC).

🧠 **NATIONAL FOOTBALL LEAGUE (NFL)**—The league that started in 1920 and is still operating today.

🧠 **PLAYOFFS**—The games played after the regular season to determine which teams play in the Super Bowl.

🧠 **PRO BOWL**—The NFL's all-star game, played after the regular season.

🧠 *PROFESSIONAL*—A player or team that plays a sport for money.

🧠 **QUARTERBACK RATING**—A special statistic that measures how well a quarterback has played.

🧠 *REPUTATION*—The way a person or a group of people is viewed by others.

🧠 **ROOKIE**—A player in his first season.

🧠 **SACKS**—Tackles of the quarterback behind the line of scrimmage.

🧠 **SUPER BOWL**—The championship of the NFL, played between the winners of the National Football Conference and American Football Conference.

🧠 *TONSILLITIS*—An infection of the tonsils, which are located in the throat.

🧠 *TRADITION*—A belief or custom that is handed down from generation to generation.

🧠 *VETERAN*—A player with great experience.

# OVERTIME

**TEAM SPIRIT** introduces a great way to stay up to date with your team! Visit our **OVERTIME** link and get connected to the latest and greatest updates. **OVERTIME** serves as a young reader's ticket to an exclusive web page—with more stories, fun facts, team records, and photos of the Packers. Content is updated during and after each season. The **OVERTIME** feature also enables readers to send comments and letters to the author! Log onto:

www.norwoodhousepress.com/library.aspx

and click on the tab: **TEAM SPIRIT** to access **OVERTIME**.

Read all the books in the series to learn more about professional sports. For a complete listing of the baseball, basketball, football, and hockey teams in the **TEAM SPIRIT** series, visit our website at:

www.norwoodhousepress.com/library.aspx

## On the Road

**GREEN BAY PACKERS**
1265 Lombardi Avenue
Green Bay, Wisconsin 54304
920-569-7500
www.packers.com

**THE PRO FOOTBALL HALL OF FAME**
2121 George Halas Drive NW
Canton, Ohio 44708
330-456-8207
www.profootballhof.com

## On the Bookshelf

To learn more about the sport of football, look for these books at your library or bookstore:

• Frederick, Shane. *The Best of Everything Football Book.* North Mankato, Minnesota: Capstone Press, 2011.

• Jacobs, Greg. *The Everything Kids' Football Book: The All-Time Greats, Legendary Teams, Today's Superstars—And Tips on Playing Like a Pro.* Avon, Massachusetts: Adams Media Corporation, 2010.

• Editors of *Sports Illustrated for Kids. 1st and 10: Top 10 Lists of Everything in Football.* New York, New York: Sports Illustrated Books, 2011.

# Index

## About the Author

**MARK STEWART** has written more than 50 books on football and over 150 sports books for kids. He grew up in New York City during the 1960s rooting for the Giants and Jets, and was lucky enough to meet players from both teams. Mark comes from a family of writers. His grandfather was Sunday Editor of *The New York Times*, and his mother was Articles Editor of *Ladies' Home Journal* and *McCall's*. Mark has profiled hundreds of athletes over the past 25 years. He has also written several books about his native New York and New Jersey, his home today. Mark is a graduate of Duke University, with a degree in history. He lives and works in a home overlooking Sandy Hook, New Jersey. You can contact Mark through the Norwood House Press website.